LET THE EMPIRE DOWN

LET THE EMPIRE DOWN

Alexandra Oliver

BIBLIOASIS
WINDSOR, ONTARIO

FIRST EDITION

Library and Archives Canada Cataloguing in Publication

Oliver, Alexandra, 1970-, author
    Let the empire down / Alexandra Oliver.

Issued in print and electronic formats.
ISBN 978-1-77196-078-6 (pbk.).--ISBN 978-1-77196-079-3 (ebook)

    I. Title.

PS8629.L54L48 2016   C811'.6   C2015-907390-1
                                             C2015-907391-X

Edited by Zachariah Wells
Copy-edited by Emily Donaldson
Typeset by Ellie Hastings
Cover designed by Kate Hargreaves

 Canada Council   Conseil des Arts    ONTARIO ARTS COUNCIL
for the Arts   du Canada   CONSEIL DES ARTS DE L'ONTARIO

 Canadian   Patrimoine
Heritage   canadien

Published with the generous assistance of the Canada Council for the Arts and the Ontario Arts Council. Biblioasis also acknowledges the support of the Government of Canada through the Canada Book Fund and the Government of Ontario through the Ontario Book Publishing Tax Credit.

PRINTED AND BOUND IN CANADA

CONTENTS

MOVIES

"I shall have to come to it—presently. But there is something else I must come to first." She paused again, trying to transmit to her voice the steadiness of her recovered smile. "There is some one I must say goodbye to. Oh, not YOU—we are sure to see each other again—but the Lily Bart you knew. I have kept her with me all this time, but now we are going to part, and I have brought her back to you—I am going to leave her here. When I go out presently she will not go with me. I shall like to think that she has stayed with you—and she'll be no trouble, she'll take up no room."

—Edith Wharton, *The House of Mirth*

THE MEGABUS GOES BY SHERBET LAKE

There's the water tank that bears its name.
There's its purple edge: the shore, the ship
that crossed the lake, beneath a heap of lime.
I went away. I gave the place the slip.

There's the mall where I would watch and wander;
there's the bench where I would go and cry;
there's the Polish deli that went under;
I left it all. It won't remember me.

There's the strip of mansions on the lee;
there's the strap that ravaged my behind.
There's the corner which they saved for me;
I made it out, and nobody will mind.

There's the pier where people disappeared;
there's the field of seven hundred crows.
The wind blows now. Convenient, ill-starred,
there it goes, forever. There it goes.

REPORT

Okay, you lot. Sit down—is what I tell them,
steering them towards the reading corner,
soft and dark, beneath *The Weather* Is
and *Birthday Friends* and *How to Be a Helper*.
Jayden, who's a handful; Faith, who totters
to her place in orchid sparkle shoes,
gentle Felix, spiderlike and shy,
Lewis, undeveloped for his age,
who likes the laser pointer. Samuel
the builder, Paul the fighter, sullen Chloë,
living with her dad since last November,
Wei-Lin, with her bright and barking laugh,
and all the rest. Those chatty dynamos
winding down together, as they clasp
each other's sweaty fingers, lean on in
the moment that I open up the book.
(I can't recall which one. Perhaps the romp
in which the stalker pushes mouldy ham
on cars, on trains, with foxes. Or the tale
in which the rolling pancake gets away.
Or the little train who thought he could, he could,
the boy who wished he wasn't made of wood,
or the other boy (papery, red-coated)
tracking pensive steps into the snow;
the story of the bunny and his father,
Hans Brinker and the pair of silver skates,
the kid who dressed himself in vulpine drag
and drove his mother nuts. That wretched tree,
who, driven by some devil, kept on giving.)

Small citizens of Thisville, twenty-three
companions, craving sweets and golden stars,
they soak the words right up, lit up and living,
their faces, hung in the corner like small moons,
around the planet of the open book.
Twenty minutes later, I arise,
(when signalled by the principal's soft knock),
walk to the door and peel away the sheet
of paper taped to block the hall's blue light,
flick the switch; the roller blinds snap up.
The bell, a bloodshot eye by the fountain,
sounds, and the world erupts in one great yell,
clunking lunch kits and the flap of jackets.
The gate clacks shut. The grey yard empties out,
the bus goes groaning off, the air turns cold,
as I look up to the blank October sun
which, looking back at me, takes aim and fires.

PREPARATORY RESEARCH

Because of all the times you've tried for jobs
in foreign places, I can name the streets
in Glasgow where the neds' maest mingin'[1] fights
take place, where some lost stripling stabs
another. I can talk about the year
the Ostrogoths took Genoa by the balls
or (in Singapore) the hawker stalls
where one can lunch on stingray and a beer.
In Athens, should you need to sell old coins,
I know the man. Southhampton has a bar
much frequented by clowns. They say the schools
in Katy, Texas are superb. The Stones
loved Oslo. What do you love? Nothing here
but us, the balcony, the view for miles.

---

1   neds' maest mingin' = hooligans' nastiest

Margaret Rose

The females of my family extolled
the virtues of our Queen, her cautious charm,
the opera glove that sheathed her guiding arm.
For this was ours, the Englishwoman's mould.

But Margaret, the microscopic-waisted,
a mantrap by the age of seventeen,
slid underneath us like a submarine,
desired, gasped at, but at last outlasted.

Her sister's pleasing properness peered out
from mugs and jugs and stamps. She had the crown.
She never stooped to let the empire down.
She never left the other sex in doubt.

But Margaret, the ruined and rapacious,
picked amongst the cricketers and rakes,
topless, fogged, a fountain of mistakes,
making cat food of noble Windsor wishes.

The E2 tank slides onward into battle,
waving stiffly from the Bentley's back,
warning certain women not to crack,
waiting for the rabble dust to settle—

while Margaret, taut and disappointed,
has sunk like squandered change into the shoals,
but in the murk, her eyes glow, purple coals.
To us, the normal, she is God's anointed.

PLANS

Mid-morning: here I sit with splayed-out hands,
womanly and worked-with, on the towel.
The manicurist, twenty at the most,
is pretty in her bow-necked carbon dress.
(The shop has not been open for a week;
a box of Thornton's Classics stands uneaten
on the table, by a copy of *Hello!*)
She has a job, Someone has told her so.
If she were made to do it, she's uncertain
(and, if she were uncertain, would she speak?).
Plucking metal clippers from a glass,
she starts to pick away, a little lost,
until the rip, the blood, the muted howl,
I'm sorry! Meaning, *Not what I had planned.*

A half an hour before, this girl had told me
how she loved her small-town school back home,
excelled in sciences, rejoiced in donning
lab coats to untuck the life from frogs,
set fire to wide-hipped flasks, lean in to watch
the magnified amoebae wink and burble
coyly in the Petri dish, a hand
unshaking on the arm of her best friend.
A girl's future should be full and bright, a marble,
but (alas for her) there is a catch:
we take on the immediate. Hope flags;
wishing to be wise and come out shining,
we pop a beaker over our own flame.
We do it cheerfully. We do it coldly.

Tamping down the soggy, trembling cotton
on my bleeding cuticle, she asks
What colour? Meaning, *How can I do better
when I know the business isn't in me?*
Look, I want to say, I've done it too,
sold candlesticks I'd never care to clean,
told women that a lipstick made them young,
gone drinking with the after-hours gang;
I've told admirers things I didn't mean
and said to students, *It'll come to you!*
The wrong direction never treats you kindly.
I long to tell her that it doesn't matter;
there's a way to live and shirk the axe,
though what that is, I've probably forgotten.

ACHIEVERS' CRADLE SONG

The neighbourhood came for that girl.
It was tucked in the cracks of the road,
and it stirred in obstreperous trees.
It climbed the infirmary walls
on the goldenrod day she was born.
She was gifted with books and with dolls,
and her parents had money to burn,
but the domovoi came in disguise.
The neighbourhood wanted that girl
and it knew she would want it as well.
She was always a curious child.

The neighbourhood waited its turn
as she raised her impeccable hand
in a seat at the front of the class,
while children from hard-bitten homes
would gape at her drawings of clouds.
It was waiting, in garrulous games,
in the hurdling shriek of the birds,
through the lessons in cello and chess.
The neighbourhood knew she'd return;
she would soon have a living to earn;
she was not above changing her mind.

The neighbourhood knew when to strike,
even after the medals for math
and the models of dungeons and ships.
She took up with a homelier foil
who set off her innocence well.
She learned how to lie and cajole;
the boys were all put through the mill
by her walk and her terrible lips.
The neighbourhood knew when to strike.
She followed it into her death.
They were both so extremely alike.

VINCENT'S MASERATI

You like the colour? Watch the way it runs,
I said to her the day I brought it home,
as slippery and shiny as a gun,
the kind of car a younger man would envy,
wishing that he'd worked a little harder
(*See what those deskbound hours were really worth?*).
I ran my hands along the bucket seats
in custard leather, dusted off the dash
and turning to her, asked if she was free,
tonight, tomorrow, for a quiet ride.
Her hair had been in rollers. I could tell,
from looking at the way it bounced. Her nails,
tipped with two good inches, painted white,
rattled, as she fiddled with her keys.
I remember when I met her in the lift
a year ago, a girl of thirty-five,
divorced, with freckled skin and lime-green eyes,
all itchy for a classy woman's world:
a kitchen with no dishes in the sink,
a wall-height window and an indoor pool,
a man who has the sense to hold his own.
And I was what she needed. If she knew
she never told me, only rapped the door
at night, to ask if I could watch the kids
or take her for a pizza. It was clear,
however, I had meaning. She would phone
a dozen times a week, for this, for that,
and every time I held her to my ear,
I had her then. I didn't feel alone

like I did, standing by the car that night.
I asked about the week ahead. She squinted,
listing off the minutes in her mind,
the hours, days, the fortnight. Said she'd see
and kissed me on the cheek. I watched her go,
sashay across the lot in unworn heels,
a pattern (parrots, ferns) around the bum
that hinted one day it might go to seed
and grow and travel south. That Jezebel.
I watched her shadow as the sun spilled red
across the tower wall. That blind gold star
is just like me, I thought. Its work won't end.
It rises, hot and heavy, and then sets.
It only wants to leave the world behind
and leave me mute with my new chariot
while time, like all the roads, runs on and on,
and every girl, when asked to choose, just runs.

CHRISTOPHER ROBIN KINDERGARTEN
CLASS PHOTO, 1974

There in the front.
That's me in the blazer
and little white hat,
already the poser,

the chin pointed up,
designing my ruse,
all set for disaster
in my red shoes.

PHOTO TAKEN BEFORE A MUGGING: FLORENCE, JULY 1976

I'm six years old, with my first leather purse
slung across my bantam-bony shoulder,
(a blue thing with a tugboat appliquéd).
It harbours neither powder, keys, nor phone,
no migraine pills, no picture of a man
I never really liked but took to bed—
just a can with seven thousand lire
(five dollars, give or take eleven cents)

I'm standing pigeon-toed in sandals, squinting,
in gingham and a gondolier's straw hat
procured at some Venetian stall. No heels,
no bored red lips, no grey roots that need doing,
no forty-something beauty that is dying.
I haven't figured out how failure feels;
unbrokenhearted, I am the astronaut
still orbiting before the dreadful landing.

THE PREDICTION

Of all my works, that which pleases me the most is the Casa that I had built in Milan to shelter elderly singers who have not been favoured by fortune, or who when they were young did not have the virtue of saving their money. Poor and dear companions of my life!
—Giuseppe Verdi

There will be no Verdi Home for you
in forty years. It isn't in the cards,
though you have always longed for phantom ships
and elephants and dirty knives and poison.
Though Pinkerton may up and sail away
at seven in the morning every day,
you've never wasted in Bartolo's prison
or let yourself expire on Tristan's lips
and, when the spotlight lands, you lack the words,
the words the music longs to fasten to.

There will be no Verdi Home tomorrow.
You won't awake to Papageno's teasing
in your brassy, lace-bedecked boudoir,
toy with your cornetti, while a fellow
(noted for his Florestan) writes letters;
no sweet-faced nurse will throw apart the shutters,
sending out the bass's dying bellow,
the duelling of the divas in the bar,
as the dirges of Orfeo, gently rising,
bring down, bring down, the curtain on his sorrow.

There will be no Verdi Home. Instead,
flat silence will descend when people call
for numbers or your eldest child's name.
And there you'll be, held captive in a ring
of baffled jackdaws wrapped in macramé,
libido, mouth, and vocal cords bone dry,
the therapist leaning in (*Come on, now! Sing!*),
the sun dissolving in its own smug flame.
You're right, you think, you're right. It is a small,
small world after all. And Verdi's dead.

Reading About Bellinghausen Island, South Sandwich Islands, After a Funeral

It's down there (somewhere), blasted form the Horn
in blurry belts of sleet and mineral grey.
Who'd want to come to see a child born?
Who'd choose to stay?

Perhaps the penguins, tiger seals and krill,
but they were here when all of this began.
They mate and mourn, collaborate and kill—
because they can.

I flick through pages. Anoraks and hoods,
crouching, taking samples, checking weather,
giving nervous scientific nods
to one another.

No sparrows settle on the station vane;
the sea's unrested and the sun's unrisen.
I wonder if it's like this where you've gone.
I hope it isn't.

WHY GIRLS NEED POETRY

In '92, I saw three illustrations.
Their subjects were the insects, born among
the many in the rubble of Chernobyl.
One was plain, a small antennaed lung,

another like a tiger-mottled shield,
a glossy thing, so vivid and so round,
whose battle duty, being legless, was
to bravely lie and wobble on the ground.

The third, pistachio and lacy pink,
had apparatus once designed for flight
that, stunted, was a petticoat half-torn.
And why do I remember them tonight,

these creatures of the great, soft, poisoned wind
that had its way with clay and putty genes
and left a blind and mouthless mass behind?
I read about the girls today, the teens

and younger, blinking in the blast
of modern times, required to be sleeker,
more desired, needed by the rest,
mandibles stretched out to clamp the weaker—

fingers rattling against their phones
berating, pleading, sprouting acronyms—
mutated stumps of meaning—limbless lines,
emoticons. Regardless of their homes,

the parents who produced them, taught them sound
as conduit for feelings, plus the books
flopped on their desks, like dying birds on sand,
they feel the DNA of speech relax

and fall apart, rebuild to monster form;
their hundred eyes and mile-extended stings
not saving them from knowing that a storm
of gentle dust has robbed them of their wings.

FEARING THE STALK

*There are those people who will always sway; they are
like crops such as rice which, because they have slender
stalks, will sway whenever the wind blows.*
—Mao Tse Tung

*Choreographed by Granny, she became the most popular
hysteric in the Virginia Hump. Men came from as far
as Leesburg to gaze into her popping eyes and grasp her
trembling hands.*
—Florence King, *Confessions of a Failed Southern Lady*

I fear I am one of those girls of the stalk.
I'm just like my mother. I tend towards shrill;
I quiver in fear of the slink in the walk,
the rubbery wretchedness stuck in my laugh,
the longing to talk on another's behalf,
the chemical urge to refuse being still.

I've seen them on telly. They like breaking down
on Oprah, drowning in soft sprays of tears.
I've seen them at Christmas, at night, taking down
their own decorations, electric with shame
or savaging neighbours' deluxe dancing flame
salvia with shouts and scissoring shears.

I've known them to shackle their hearts to campaigns,
buzzing with wrath, a professional wreck,
and fading to black with the pulse of their veins,
appalled by the slight of a personal wrong
or relatives failing to jolly along
an albatross, slumped on the family deck.

Where is my river of ladylike chill,
my Eleanor Roosevelt life-giving salt,
compassion for suffering, brute iron will,
or Mary-of-Egypt immaculate eye,
bathed in the net of the messaging sky,
as secret and true as a fireproof vault?

I could be like a dancer from Chinese Ballets,
all banners and fists and empowering look,
all muscular, future-directed jetés.
But they had their share of the stalk girls, I bet,
(the prima, propped up on her black bayonet:
Which one of you whores has my Little Red Book?).

THE REUNION

In families, they say, there's always one:
the child who spills his milk, as if on cue.
He is the one you put your love into
and, once you stop, you're broken and undone.

You watch him shove his brother on the stairs,
grip the hamster with a tightening hand,
complain, complain, complain to beat the band,
march like a majorette right though your prayers.

And how can you forget him, when you leave
to run around the block, float in a pool,
get a facial? Soon, you'll hear that howl;
you'll never make it out of him alive.

When he's grown, you get the same advice:
he needs to eat less sugar, have a minder.
He's one of those who'll never let you wander
or love another more. Remember this.

Of course it's *right* that he be here today
even as his eye consumes the child
who lingers by the exit, unconcealed,
the nanosecond that you turn away.

Diagnosis

And this is you at six a.m.:
the silver clouds are brewing,
your lower limbs resemble ham,
your charms are all ungluing.
You're haemorrhaging radiance;
your blood is low on perfect—
try telling folks they loved you once.
Take care, because you're worth it.

THE LITTLE MACHINES

This is the bird we love
in the gold cage.
Turning the key and waiting
(coming of age,

knowing it's old and precious
those feathers, that tar-black beak),
we set the cage down and listen.
For an antique,

how fine it is at singing,
turning its gilded throat,
soaring in both directions
on the same note;

the eyes don't tear or blink
as the bright wings click and rustle;
over the black felt mat
the gears sigh and whistle.

The bird's intelligent voice
betrays no vital despair.
It will break, rather than die.
It doesn't care.

Two Roads
After Dura Jakšić

From where I stand, two paths roll out ahead:
one is filled with flowers, one with thorn.
As I wear armour, I will dare to tread
the rougher path, back to where I was born.

The blooming way before me I bestow
upon the meek, the weak, the poor, the tender.
It is for them the fickle flowers grow;
the thorns alone belong to their defender.

MIHIZ

After Matija Bećković

I haven't been out in a very long time
or seen anybody (nor will I tomorrow).
I lost all my hobbies. I don't give a damn.
I don't even bother to look out the window.

So why don't you take yourself off to some prison—
Sremska Mitrovica, Zabela, say—
sit in for some wearied and cagey old felon
who'd give his left nut to escape for one day,

even if only to wander the streets
or gape like a dope in the warmth of the sun?

But friend, aren't I pacing my cell in defeat
when somebody else had the courage to run?

THE SIGNAL

At seven, it's a town of lighthouse keepers.
They wake and stand at windows. When they leave,
(beneath a sky that leaks on dogs and sweepers)
buttoning coats, grinning and alive,
they saunter past the tenements to schools
or jobs, living as tinder sparked from stone.
Some beacon within them must be seen for miles
by those white ships down south which drift alone.

Entertaining the Locals

They come at you, without a word of warning,
bullhorn-voiced, their hands clamped on your arm,
intent on dinner, though they wish you harm.
They breach your home. You smell the sulfur burning.
You cannot bear their kids, their dumpling wives,
the questions on your hair, your fear, your war.
Beware the bottle that they bring, the store
they recommend, the island-knitted gloves
they give for Christmas. Try to flee and fail—
they'll get you to the bar, the match, the track,
exotic, unprepared, your weapons scarce.
They will not stop until you tell your tale,
drink until you weep and like them back,
put money on a worried-looking horse.

KELVINBRIDGE, GLASGOW, 2 P.M.

Look below: the sable-eddied Kelvin
flowing fast, despite the town's depression;
never angry, only bloody-minded,
rolling on to reach the red horizon.

Glaswegians put their trust in how it carries:
they toss into its care the things they use:
lolly sticks and condoms, knives and bottles,
babies' toys, a jilted lover's shoes.

A force that churns has somewhere else to be,
especially when spattered with this light.
Someone got it started; it is free.
To go a little closer must be right.

And sometimes there's a child from an estate
pulled from games along the muddy edge,
and this is why the branches bend and wait
and why we always pause upon this bridge.

TRADING

Ten minutes left to go until the bell.
I see you as you sit and dole your stash
while twenty of your clients squirm and watch
against the piss- and poster-plastered wall.

To me they're only millionaires in shorts,
four-inches high, released from foil packs,
but watching Rooney leave your hands for Becks,
van Persie for Buffon, I'll say it smarts,

that image of you on a crowded floor,
shouting at a ticker board, your tie
askew. Or in a basement, mute and grey,
before a bank of screens. Or there's the blur

of passengers emerging from a bus,
the gentle slipping of a bag of green
into a student's purse, the constant rain,
the counted cash. I am afraid of this.

I want the you that loved the plastic barn
and horses, coloured, glorified Darth Vader.
The mother of a trader knows that later
something is exacted in return.

THE VANISHING

The rain is falling because it's bored.
You find a sandwich in the bed.
The drunks are wailing in the park.
The car is waiting in the shop.
Your only friend's about to snap:
her husband shagged a girl from work.
She took her son and hit the road.
She'll never call again. It's hard.

The road uphill is getting longer.
The friendly building crew is gone;
a block of flats squats in their place.
The peach-faced brick won't smoke or laugh
or whistle Polish songs of love,
but none of it has gone to waste
and here, between the shit and stone,
a crocus gives the rain the finger.

THE BALLAD OF LOCKERBIE

The children went out to the fields one night
when the hoarfrost had lacquered the trees.
Their hair was all copper, their skin was all white;
they were seen by the Maid of the Seas.

The Maid had an eye that glowed in the cold
and hands like flame-coloured wings;
she scattered the fields with silver and gold,
with nickels and shekels and rings

and buttons from blazers and monogrammed racks
for toast and the buckles from shoes
and zippers and fillings and delicate forks,
and the children, with ah's and with ooh's,

dove on their knees for the shower of wealth
and loaded their pockets with cheers,
but the foxes and hares caught the odour of death
and bolted, with quivering ears.

The hamlet that shimmered, way up on the hill,
knew nothing of what lay ahead,
with infants to feed and ovens to fill
and cordwood to stack in the shed.

The Maid of the Seas shook her china-blue skirts
and swooped down, like an eagle, below,
and the village dissolved in a billion parts,
and the night was as quiet as snow.

And the children were led to a house on the moor
that belonged to the Maid of the Seas,
who ushered them in before closing the door,
which she locked with a charred set of keys.

OPEN-ENDED

The train rattles on to Shettleston,
and the caravans crouch on the overfed grass
while schooners of washing flap in the sun
(uniforms, sheets, a cheap yellow dress).
A titan emerges and walks to the swings,
shedding a sweater and flicking his ashes.
The child is waiting, all braids and white lashes,
a gumdrop in gumboots. She springs and she sings
as the man stoops down to the chains and pushes.

The train rattles on to Shettleston
and someone's been dead for over three years.
When you get past the worst, you can be someone;
you can rattle along when the avalanche clears.
Outside, in the blue, like an exclamation,
a jetliner's trail marks the getaway climb,
leaving you in the carriage, exalted and lame,
to examine the ticket you bought at the station,
which tells you, or someone, *Return: anytime.*

THE WORKER

That's the one. The girl who gives him grief,
who nestles at his elbow, streaks the ink
across his shaky page of sums, pulls rank
with lisping whispers: *faggot, liar, thief,*
I'm going to cut you up. They dish the dirt
at parent-teacher meetings: broken home,
a missing dad, the system is to blame.

But know the act of acting out's an art
not hoarded by the people of this street.
I've seen it trickle through the sunset lawns
back home, where golden women come together,
gimlet-eyed, for barbecues and gin
while, at the table, sweet in her young bones,
a freckled fawn, gracile as her mother,
decapitates a spider with her pen.

BOSSES

They're the ones who pointed out the door,
said you were unproductive, wrong, disliked.
Once it was done, you feared them even more:
some wigged-out wraith, escaping underfloor,
the vampire hunter with a hawthorn spike.

You have to broach the wretched, month-past task,
approach them in their high, expelling seat,
jerk your sagging breastbone in and ask
for references, insults in a mask:
"Tried very hard." "Good hygiene." "Pleasant." "Neat."

Why is it that we fear the stinging switch,
now closeted and curling in a box,
avoid them at the trade show with a twitch,
abandoning the old and vengeful itch
to sail on, with a tossing of one's locks?

Warm yourself with them, a blanket shell,
wrap them tightly round your frozen flanks;
hear their muffled, sad, hypoxic swell
as they go shooting down to that bright hell
where someone shuts their file and says, *No thanks.*

GROCERY SKIPPING SONG

Butter. Sugar. Flour. Water.
Penne. Tuna. Kitchen paper.
There's a man in aisle seven
with his girl against the shelving.
I can hear *You bitch, you better.*
(Whiskey. Hammer. Pepper shaker.)
When I look a little closer,
I can see he dreams of murder.
(Brisket. Bucket. Lino cleaner.)
I can see he wants to hit her.

Who's in charge if he won't do it?
(Jell-O. Fairy. Cotton batting.)
She won't listen ever, dammit.
(Red Bull. Roses. Bug repellant.)
Does he, does he? Does he do it?
Move along, the guard will mutter.
(Scratch for savings, only Monday.)
Stop him, speak, I'll do it one day;
I check out on someone's daughter;
Butter. Sugar. Flour. Water.

THE VILLAINS
For D.L.

I always went for darkness as a girl:
those ashy Europeans wrapped in capes,
glazed ranks of zombies browsing in the mall,
the cabin-dwelling fan with swelling hopes,

her novelist in reach. I don't know why
I leaned toward the viper in the mink,
the tortured trader in the Charvet tie,
lancet primed to disembowel the bank.

Bad, so bad, a shudder more than human—
when will we see their dreadful likes again,
the drips who mapped the older starlets' ruin
or herded virgins into wicker men,

the hazmat-suited soldiers, come for you,
the porkpie preacher targeting the young,
for hidden money, crossing the bayou,
white knuckles flashing "love" and "hate"? How come?

Could it be that daybreak lay ahead
with sunny buses, clinking streams of coins,
the people taking lunches, nearly dead,
waiting for their sandwiches in lines,

that muttering backs were hovering in bars,
that children were deciding what to leave,
that cubicles had manacles and ears—
and you, with nothing left to do but drive

toward the setting sun, your rosebud home,
the neighbours you can't fathom or forgive,
then up the stairs to the crib in the back room
containing something awful and alive.

WATCHING THE COP SHOW IN BED

Apparently, it's very, very bad
to let a well-dressed man into your home.
An Oxbridge accent, coupled with the claim
your husband's hurt, and he's from Scotland Yard:
disaster! He'll thunk and chloroform you, drag
you off at knifepoint to his boat,
exsanguinate your body, write some smut
from Crowley on the walls, then eat your leg.

He'll leave the rest of you inside a freezer,
to be discovered by a sad detective
bellowing, *we made it here too late!*

Too late indeed. I used to feel wiser,
more in charge, a little more creative.
Now, like the rest, I watch the door and wait.

TEST RESULTS

Near misses: I can say I've had too many:
Thomas in his leopard-skin and chaps;
Eric of the attitude, his hips
rounding out the vowels of Shirley Bassey;
Paolo, in that Washington hotel,
begging to be beaten. Chubby Victor
(socialist) who sent expansive letters
weekly, when I was at uni. It's well
and good to sow one's seed, but walking home,
the doctor's word's as welcome as a lamp
creeping through a cave to sunlight, outside,
away from unformed You, the rush, the game,
the bearing of bad news, the arms gone limp,
and all those phone calls waiting to be made.

HOW BEAUTIFUL IS NIGHT
For R. T., 1967–2013

For the record; there's a record that I love
because you loved it too (before you died).
That night you told me that I shouldn't leave
and I'd be better off with you instead,

you put on George Shearing. Rumour says
his contracts gave him final right to choose
the models on the front of his LPs
though he was blind. I kicked my green silk shoes

beneath the bed, as Farnon's strings ballooned
with cruel and tender schmaltz. A gauzy sleeve,
the harp came in a flutter and was gone.
And then the master entered. Who'd believe

the way the keys could cut a trail through
the smugness of a twentysomething mind?
Seventeen years on, I can't undo
the way it feels. Pianos are unkind.

I turn the cover in my hands and linger:
there is no lounging, sloe-eyed femme fatale
in satin, but a London bridge in winter.
You've crossed I hear. How beautiful. That's all.

JOB PROPOSAL FOR GAVRA, AGED SEVEN, WHO HAS BEEN GIVEN A 452-PAGE SCIENCE ALMANAC

Today, while going to the shops, you told
your dad and me about the tapeworm's cycle,
how each untested pork chop means survival.
Thrilled to teach, you would not be controlled.
We got the full meal deal; you had the feeding
habits down: the scolex seeking tenure
in the gut's sweet fleshy, floral pasture,
the weight loss, faintness, and suspicious bleeding.
Next time we're in a room of lurching bores
discussing stocks or Taylor Swift's last show
or why their past liaisons never jelled,
I'll pay you fifty bucks for three whole hours
to tell the buggers everything you know
(plus bonus, when the last one is expelled).

YOUR TURN
For G.B.

Dad liked games with *master* in the title:
Mastermind (where players have to guess
the colours of a screened-off row of brittle
plastic pegs. In half a minute (less!)

he broke the code, being blessed with a knack
for knowing what particulars stay hidden—
its origins in algorithm, luck,
and serving in Intelligence for Britain),

and Parker Brothers' Masterpiece (which fanned
the art collector's lust. An auctioneer
would take our bids. We clamoured, cash in hand,
for treasures, over Van Gogh's board-flat stare.

He redesigned his background and his class
through stacking up on Hopper, Blume, and Wood,
alertly sensing what one could possess
securely and which beauty was a fraud).

Now he's gone, it's my turn to convey
to you that our survival's tied to guessing,
knowing what abundance fools the eye
and keeping at it when the rules go missing.

MOVIES

CINEMA, OPEN CITY

Look down. Look at Rome as it opens its gates. I was there.
I was there when the priest at the desk would not crack,
when the innkeeper's wife threw the drifter a bone,
when the rice planters sheltered and tutored the crooks;
I was there when the bicycle's theft brought despair,
when dogs followed masters to hell and then back,
made them move from the path of oncoming trains. I was there.

Step out. Step into the sun without fear. I was more
on the Finzi-Continis' delectable grass,
believing the daughter would love on forever,
the warmth on the handles of rackets remaining.
I was more, when a sad Polish boy on the shore,
faded into the mist, faded into the past,
and carried the marvelling crowd on his wings. I was more.

Bear up. Bear up, when it all makes no sense. I became
something else when the woman out sailing went missing,
when the elegant prince saw the stormy horizon,
its eddies in petticoats, pipe smoke, and lilies.
Something else when the journalist smothered his shame
in a fountain, with someone too starry for kissing;
the cinema burned, and the child who returned I became.

Come in. Come into the room and the light. We are here
with the Pope who won't Pope to his ultimate breath,
with the tourists, unhinged, in the manic piazzas,
up to our elbows in sausage and cheese,
with the banker as Judas, the fisherman's spear,
with the cousin—a bullet now faster than death.
In the light, here tonight, we converge, we begin. We are here.

THE EVENT

The town has been struck with a case of Fellini:
women in feathers, in fountains, on phones,
in pasties, on ponies, with warm golden trumpets,
sinister, innocent, ripe to their bones.

The fascists are crowding the parks with the oxen,
which paw at the hems of the socialites' gowns.
You can't get a taxi for love or for money;
the lot have been taken by bishops and clowns.

My mother's been compromised by Casanova,
the man that I love has ascended a tree
and is screaming for women: Anouk or Anita
or anyone more European than me.

A pimp by a river has taken my purse;
my husband insists that I visit the Pope;
the neighborhood nympho won't budge from my window.
It's all gone to hell. And will stay there, I hope.

LO SCIECCO BIANCO

"Lei è graziosa, dolce, e piccolina…"

Wanda: she is graceful, sweet, and teeny.
Problem is, she's missing. In a boat
somewhere, without her matron's camel coat,
she wriggles from the kisses of a genie:

Nando, crimson-lipped and double-chinned,
a rippling wave of sequins, chest hair, gold.
But, after vicious wives and biting cold,
she makes it home, a butterfly repinned.

Her husband, Ivan, saucer-eyed protector,
having wrestled porters, cops, and whores,
reclaims his Wanda, graceful, sweet, and teeny.

Thank God these youngsters had the right director;
(the id directed through the back room doors).
Thank God it didn't go to Pasolini.

LA DOLCE VITA

The Christ that I know is a statue en route to the Pope.
The woman I live with has circled my neck with a rope.
Her love comes to me on a ripple of promise and pills;
from here to the end of the week is its own seven hills,
and hope is an heiress spread out on a hooker's divan,
and time stretches out like a hand to the wrong drowning man.

Love, love, and love are the words from an actress's mouth,
and how do I show her the way that we love in the south?
I tell her my home is in her, as the fountain roars on.
She tosses her terrible Valkyrie head and is gone;
to her I'm a joke, with the requisite teeth and a tan,
and time stretches out like a hand to the wrong drowning man.

The Virgin is sighted, the cameras flash like the sun,
but what does it mean when the best of all men are undone?
My friend, on a quest for the truth in the tract and the song,
takes off on eternal sabbatical. Maybe it's wrong,
but most of his cosmic supporters say run while you can,
and time stretches out like a hand to the wrong drowning man.

The angels are trumpeting sadly amid the balloons;
they dish up risotto at tables that border the dunes.
They hold up their hands in a tenderness tinged with regret,
but I will stay close to my worst and the beast in my net.
Making it out of this place is not part of the plan
and time stretches out like a hand to the wrong drowning man.

8 ½ (OTTO E MEZZO)

Maya, let's entertain these bores!
We'll make a movie! Easier than falling
off a health-spa bench. It is my calling—
phone that rocket-builder friend of yours!

Now I'm awake, the meaning is so clear.
I have no guilt about my thousand flings,
my parents lost. I have regained my wings;
I soar, upon the engines of my fear.

Yes, this is a tribute to my life;
no, there is no patent Marxist theme;
yes, I saw you sitting in the steam.
No, I will not cast your teenaged wife.

Who knows about the waters of this source?
Who wants to come and dance before my whip?
Who dares to give the cardinal the slip?
Who cares about your Mexican divorce?

So, joyfully, I let the critics down,
and this is how I honour you tonight:
I let my loved ones dance, aloft in white,
imprisoned in a holy martyr's crown.

SATYRICON

In old Rome, as Fellini explains,
the men were all oversexed swains
who lusted for underage swains
in miniature loincloths and capes;
a woman was panned for her brains,
and poets were pelted with grapes.

LA STRADA

For sale with lorry: strongman, 6-foot-1,
monobrowed, broad-shouldered, smoker, white,
village-fierce, unrivalled in a fight,
net weight last pulled with chain and teeth: one ton.
Anger management is recommended.
Bad with pets and acrobats. Alone.
When clean and sober, stoic as a stone.
Known to have been loved, but not befriended.
Good for drawing crowds (present with drum).
Groom with greatest flattery and guile;
use caution when a crowbar is in sight.
But most of all, when recollections come,
refrain from trumpets and a certain smile.
Above all else: protect from beach and night.

On Michael Haneke's *The White Ribbon*

Eichwald, Germany, 1914

In the village of the silver sun
the cabbages grow fat, a woman sweeps
the vestry steps, the choir meets to sing
and, in this ring of dust, the ogre sleeps.

Beware the hand that wanders to caress,
the rotting planks stacked on the sawmill floors,
the river reeds, the gentle baroness,
the rugs, the glass, the brass, the basement doors.

The feudal son has learned to carve a flute
for what? It will not stop the switch's bite.
The doctor's girl has opals for her ears
provided he can visit her at night.

And so, the children glide from house to house;
they hover under windows, blank as bone,
transparent lashes fluttering. They ask
no favours, just (they say) to help their own.

In the village of the silver sun
the blinded, blank, abandoned hear a shot
that echoes round the world. A silver gun
that promises to rescue them—or not.

ON WONG KAR-WEI'S *IN THE MOOD FOR LOVE*

The woman is a column of despair.
Though coiffed and bright and practical, she glides
through alleyways. One evening she collides
with Him. Do not imagine an affair
will happen. There will only be the stroll
towards the noodle seller, or the fan
that sighs above their shoulders. When they can,
they chat about the serials, recall
the purse of one, the necktie of the other
(the lines of each recall the spouses missing;
missing something has become routine).
Neither knows what brought them here together,
but look: beside two pairs of warm hands pressing,
the coffee shivers in its melamine.

SUSPIRIA

I hear the sliding door's hydraulics sighing,
Do it then. The wall of beating rain
as biblical a caveat as Cain
(without the garden or the brother dying).

Dying: why is now the time to fear it,
now, when blindly waving at the grills
of taxis, I can see the gilded sills
of hell below? I know that we are near it.

Near it, near the driver's sullen head
that will not turn around to my distress
but only steers his Benz to that address
without a word. Are all these Germans dead?

Dead, the branches of the livid trees;
the shadows come enraged and disappear.
The dancing school approaches; we are here.
I run, the wind roars like a swarm of bees,

like bees. I see a woman; panic-stung,
she flies and staggers back into the wood.
Will she escape? From what? And, if she could,
they'll get her later. Pity. She is young.

Young, like me. The heroine must find,
unearth the secrets of the crimson hall.
It is my job—or why come here at all
and leave the safe and gentle ones behind?

Behind me were those I lived for pleasing,
parents in white houses, passion-poor
and so, I throw myself at this red door,
its hell-hot handle. Let me. I am freezing.

ACKNOWLEDGEMENTS

EARLIER VERSIONS OF THESE POEMS were published in the following magazines and literary journals: *The Walrus, Light, Partisan, Canadian Notes & Queries, The New Guard* (*BANG!* Poet feature section), *Mezzo Cammin, The Raintown Review,* and *White Coffee.* "Grocery Skipping Song" and "Margaret Rose" (which made its first appearance in *The Walrus*) were published, respectively, in the anthologies *Measure for Measure* (Random House/Everyman 2015) and *Best Canadian Poetry 2015* (Tightrope Books 2015). My gratitude goes out to the editors.

"The Event," "Lo Sciecco Bianco," "La Dolce Vita," "8 ½," and "Satyricon" were commissioned as part of a series for the Spectacular Obsessions Fellini Retrospective at the TIFF Bell Lightbox in Toronto in June 2011.

There would be no book without the support—logistical and emotional—of everyone at Biblioasis. Thanks are due to the following brave souls: Bennett Aron, Matijia Beckovic, Kim Bridgford, Justine Brown, Pino Coluccio, D. Lawrence, Rachel Lebowitz, Michael Lista, Guy Maddin, all the Olivers in Vancouver, Molly Peacock, and George Szirtes. And finally, love and gratitude is due in spades to those mighty men in the wings, Dragan and Gavra.

ALEXANDRA OLIVER WAS BORN in Vancouver, BC. Her last book, *Meeting the Tormentors in Safeway* (Biblioasis 2013), was the recipient of the 2014 Pat Lowther Memorial Award. Oliver is the co-editor (with Annie Finch) of *Measure for Measure: An Anthology of Poetic Meters* (Random House/Everyman 2014) as well as a co-editor of Canadian formalist journal *The Rotary Dial*, and a contributing editor for both *Partisan* and *ARC Poetry*. She lives in Burlington, Ontario.